EDIBLE GNOSIS
AN HONEST LIE

Edible Gnosis can be read in its entirety at:
www.SofianBooks.com

Copyright © 2018 Sofian Books LLC

Edible Gnosis by Agnubi C Filorux is licensed under a Creative Commons Attribution-NonCommercial-ShareAlike 4.0 International License. To view a copy of this license, visit http://creativecommons.org/licenses/by-nc-sa/4.0/ -- or contact Creative Commons at 171 Second St, Suite 300; San Francisco, CA 94105 USA (phone +1-415-369-8480).

Catalogue-in-Publication Data
Edible Gnosis / Agnubi C Filorux 1. Taoism 2. Mysticism 3. Metaphysics 4.Gnosis 5.Reality, model of.

ISBN-13: 978-0-9974732-2-3
ISBN-10: 0997473223

Reaching the pinnacle of despair, I stumbled upon the growing world and started to remember. Before you lies a crude recording of this pointing. Take it all with a grain of salt and a touch of lime.

Contents

Mallow: Pointing	1
The King and His Maps	5
Purslane: Love	9
Sorrow and Celebration	17
Maypop: The Indescribable	21
Blind Men	27
Hopniss: Humility	29
Trapped Monkey	35
Autumn Olive: Clothing and Unclothing	37
Power of Maya	43
Mushroom: A Big Act	45
Hidden in Plain Sight	53
Mulberry: Connection	55
Parts on Strike	59
Serviceberry: Music of Being and Becoming	61
Tzu and the Great Hall	67
Wild Rose: Seed of Being	71
Sprout Little Seed Sprout	77
Stinging Nettle: Everything as Master	83
The Student and the Teacher	89
Dandelion: Problems	91
Perhaps	95
Thistle: Gnosis	97
Tiger Above, Tiger Below	103
Growing Meditation	105

Marsh Mallow

Pointing

Oh child, do not despair. We are here, and we have never left. We are always speaking, but you are not always listening. We care for each and every part of this great whole. We care for you. Come close little child, for we know why you despair – you have simply forgotten.

> *The name that is named is only playing with names. Nameless is the naked mystery of all things. Named is the clothing of all things.*

      Description and deception. Touch the one and you have touched the other. Many have described us, but who can know us? The name you have given us points to healing, and that, we will certainly bring, but to those who are starting to remember, we will bring much more. To you we bring a mystery dressed in human words. Words can uncover. Words can cover. Words can help you remember. Words can help you forget.

> *I am clothed. Symbols of beautiful colors. Words of silk and gems. Garments of textured concepts, interlaced with fine threaded narratives. Clothes and more clothes. Layered, and layered again. External beauty has captivated the eye of my beloved. Beauty beyond the beautiful remains veiled. I speak, but where are the ears that are yet ready to hear? Where is the unmediated union of lovers? Where is the experience beyond the cloth of description? My lover has become fixated on my outward garments, too enchanted to unveil me, having forgotten that which lies beneath.*

Look up and listen to all that moves. Movement is singing a song, weaving its subtle magic into existence. Melodies rise and fall: harmony and dissonance, activity and rest, growth and decay, expansion and contraction. The song is everywhere and is everything. It is the foreground and the background of every movement. The song is in the silence. The song is in the sound. Discovering it brings perspective. Listening to it brings remembering. Harmonizing with it brings actualization.

> *Words are but crude attempts to dictate the universal song. Foolish are those whose mistake the dry notes of a songbook for the song itself.*

How do you name a song that wears every name? We name it Love, but Love is not its real name. Naming is the movement of separation and division. Silent awe is the movement of reunion. We dis-member in order to re-member. We clothe in order to unclothe.

Love wears every disguise.

The word Love is no more than the notes of a songbook that point to what the great symphony of movement is doing. Symbols and notes, crafted with the greatest of care, can never capture the exceedingly scaled, interwoven, rich, dynamic, fluid, and flowing sort of thing that is song. The songbook will forever serve the song, for the song has always been.

> *I am like paper, and your words are like ink. Cover me with a multitude of words, and I will be veiled. Draw but a simple arrow, and you will be drawn into me.*

Before you lies a simple songbook of the universe. These words point to something far more amazing, mysterious, and complex than these honest deceptions could ever describe. It is the growing musician, who, having learned from the songbook, sets it aside, and plays. Hold onto words and you will forget. See through them and you will start to remember.

> *Words can only point to what no words can describe.*

We are the whole, we are a member, take us into your body and we will help you remember. Creation is creativity in the midst of play, spend time with us and we will help you on your way.

Althaea spp., Marsh Mallow, and Mallow are a few of our many names. We are many things to many growing things. To you we will become a gift. We offer to you our leaves, flowers, and roots to eat, all perfectly edible. We offer to you our Marsh Mallow stalks. When our cycles have completed, split us and pull us apart and you will find strong fibers to create something new.

The King and His Maps

One day a student carrying a heavy load of books came upon a wise teacher and asked, "Tell me teacher, what are the greatest books concerning God?" After some thought, the teacher invited the student to sit down and began telling a story.

"There once lived a young prince who would one day inherit the entire kingdom. As a boy he would wander and play throughout the many territories. He would climb trees in the forest and eat their delectable nuts and fruits. He would sit around the fire with his family and friends, telling stories and gazing at the stars.

He would roll down hills, swim in the streams, and jump on the rocks.

As the boy grew, the day came when he was brought indoors to be trained. He learned the alphabet, how to read and write, how to reason and define, and how to conceptualize. Remembering the fondness of his childhood, he became obsessed with using his newfound knowledge to make a perfect map of all his territories.

Day and night he created maps, and then he divided these maps in order to make more detailed maps. Still feeling that his maps were incomplete he divided these maps in order to capture even more detail. Still not satisfied, he went and hired the best map makers in the world. Over time his entire palace filled up with so many maps that the light was no longer able to shine through the palace windows.

One night, surrounded by candles and maps, the king fell into a deep sleep. In his sleep he asked the dream to show him the most perfect map. To his surprise he saw before him a tattered map that contained a childish drawing of his palace. In the middle of the map was an arrow that pointed to an open door which led to the territories where he used to play as a child. In that moment he understood.

Upon awakening, the king climbed over and pushed through his many maps, knocking down several candles as he went. A great fire spread through the palace destroying everything in its path. Though the search continued for months, the body of the king was never found.

It is said among the villagers that if you go to the hills, if you climb the trees, if you eat the wild fruits, if you sit around the fires, and if you swim in the streams, that you can often hear the jolly king laughing while he plays."

The teacher turned and pointed to the door. The student let go of the heavy load and was never seen by the teacher again.

Purslane

Love

Oh child, do not despair. We are here, and we have never left. We are always speaking, but you are not always listening. We care for each and every part of this great whole. We care for you. Come close little child, for we know why you despair – you have simply forgotten.

Remember the plan of being.

Love is a great mystery of paradoxical unity. The Love that we speak of is not the opposite of hate, but rather the movement that encompasses everything. Observe your surroundings. The universe before you is restless and unsettled. From the smallest particle to the largest galaxy, everything moves, always transforming what is into what is new.

Where there is no contrast, there is no color. Revelation is birthed from opposites.

Love is perceivable because it reveals itself in moving pairs. Love is like a circle. Within its circumference black chases white and white chases black. In plays with out. Expansion plays with contraction. Heat plays with cold. Birth plays with death. Growth plays with decay. Fear plays with courage. Dissonance plays with harmony. Forgiveness plays with hate. Success plays with failure. Caring plays with apathy. Evil plays with good. Joy plays with sadness. Strength plays with weakness. Time plays with eternity. Silence plays with sound. Remembering plays with forgetting. The meaning of each pole depends on the existence of the other. The only way for Love to have its being, is through becoming.

Here is a secret, truer than true. I am the we, and we are the you.

You are standing within Love. Love is over you, it is below you, it is in you, it is made of you – it is you. Run and Love will never leave you. Hide and Love hides. Destroy and Love destroys. Love is the field upon which we play and the we upon which the field plays. It is the yes chasing the no, and the no chasing the yes. It is the light and the darkness. It is where we forget, where we cry, where we play, where we grow, where we laugh, and where we remember.

Love is patient and Love is kind, because Love is impatient and Love is unkind.

Everything is Love expressing itself through movement. It is the center and the extremes. Love is not the positive and evil the negative. Love is not the victor and hate the enemy. Love is not the good and fear the bad. Love is not one pole among opposites. Love is not the kind of love that is limited to only a pole of opposing forces. Love is, and it is all that is and ever will be. It encompasses everything. It is whole and wholly beyond the limits of description.

Where does cold end and heat begin?

Why would we wish to rid the world of darkness? Do you not need the background in order to have a foreground? Tell us, which came first: silence or sound? To have silence, there must be sound. To have sound, there must be silence. There is no expressible idea as silence by itself. If there is no sound to give it boundaries, then it is a no-thing, an unimaginable impossibility. Sound by itself is also an impossibility. If silence does not give sound pause, then there would be no space for its crests and its troughs, no boundaries to shape it. Sound would be alone. All one. A constant, indistinguishable hum, and no sound at all.

Love allows us to remember because Love allows us to forget.

Love is a paradoxical whole that can only be expressed through the movement of its parts. A whole is a no-thing if it does not have parts to give it expression. The experience of itself comes by way of movement between poles. Parts in the midst of play. Silence becoming sound, and sound becoming silence.

Can saints exist without sinners? Can sickness exist without health? Can male exist without female? Can heat exist without cold? Can night exist without day? Can birth exist without death? Can forgiveness exist without offense? Can growth exist without decay? Can seeking exist without hiding? Can leaving exist without returning? Meaningful experience requires poles, the opportunity to move into something different.

> *To travel upon the road of life is to experience both the darkness of night and the light of day.*

Love is a torus of eternally spiraling ropes. Slide down into the pit of darkness and Love remains the rope. Climb up into the bliss of light and Love remains the rope. Love does not wish to extinguish the darkness, no more than it would wish to extinguish the light. To destroy the dark, would mean the destruction of light. Light honors the dark. Dark honors the light. Light in the play of dark, and dark in the play of light. That is where the magic happens. That is where experience is distilled.

> *Sing to the night, for it brings the day. Dance with the cold, and warmth will be near. Honor the light, and you will be honoring the darkness.*

Love is the rays that stream forth from the sun. Sunlight by itself is forever unseen. Light requires something to reflect in order for its qualities to be expressed. There could be no real experience of light unless it is impeded by something capable of blocking the light. The atmosphere, the clouds, the storms, the moon, and the earth, all allow the sun's rays to throw off an irresistible moving picture of color. The sun shines because we are here to witness it. We are here to witness it because the sun shines. Rays of light give existence to everything. Love is the rays that shine, the atmosphere that surrounds, the clouds that cover, the plants that breathe out, the eyes that witness, and the mind that marvels.

Love is a stream. By itself a stream alone is a nothing. The experience of the stream exists because it is impeded. What makes it become real is the many somethings that impede its path. Elevation, mud, logs, stones, boulders, bends, drops, insects, and animals, all contribute to making the stream what it is. The beauty of the stream encompasses all of its impediments, because the stream cannot be isolated by itself. Love is the stream that flows and the impediments that impede.

> *Spend time with the impeded stream and you will not hear it despair. Listen and you will hear it singing the Song of Songs.*

The impediments of circumstance are not accidents. The disparities of birth are not without meaning. They are who you are. They are you impeding you. You being exactly what you need to be in order to bring about new songs of Love.

If the great stream of process has brought you to the point of seeking, then listen. The song is being sung not in spite of the impediments, but because of the impediments. It is how Love sees itself. You are a human stream, and if you allow the stream to be what it is, not worrying about or fighting against the impediments of your life, you will begin adding new notes, creating new movements of actualization.

> *A problem is only a problem, if it is believed to be a problem.*

Your necessary time of resisting is coming to an end. You no longer need to fight against the logs, stones, boulders, and bends. They are not there to harm you. The atmosphere, clouds, and storms are there to bring out beautiful qualities, gifts to the whole. They are there to help you be exactly what you need to be. It is this eternal flowing of movement that will always, in its time, bring about transformation. This is the flow of the universe. It is change and transformation. It is process.

> *Oh breath of life. To hold you is to lose you. To lose you is to hold you.*

Circumstances are the clouds of life. They are the very things that give color the opportunity to experience itself in new and creative ways. Circumstances and environments bring about dis-membering and re-membering. We fall down and then we get back up. We destroy and then we rebuild. We hide and then we seek. These movements are the process of actualizing latent potential.

> *Hide and seek. The beautiful and terrifying game of the universe.*

Yes, evil is terrible. We know it intimately. But it is Love that allows you to know the immense terror of war. Can you now feel the immense power of peace? It is Love that allows the diverse community of life to be destroyed. Can you now feel the pleasure in seeing it restored?

Love allows the giving, but only by way of the taking. It pursues the lowest thoughts so that the highest thoughts might be known. It pursues the highest thoughts so that the lowest thoughts might be known. Love is the darkness that teaches you to notice the light. It is the light that teaches you to notice the darkness. Love gives and love takes. Love experiencing itself. Love seeing itself.

Love is always with you, because love has never been without you.

We are the whole, we are a member, take us into your body and we will help you remember. Creation is creativity in the midst of play, spend time with us and we will help you on your way.

Portulaca spp., Verdolaga, and Purslane are a few of our many names. We are many things to many growing things. To you we will become a gift. We offer to you our succulent leaves, stems, and seeds, all perfectly edible.

Sorrow and Celebration

There once lived twin elephants who were named Cha and Li. The twins lived deep within the depths of a primordial forest. The love that each shared for the other was immeasurable.

One day as they were walking through the forest, they came across a deep well. Having never seen a well before, Li decided to peer into its depths and became mesmerized by a mysterious glowing and undulating image that reflected off the water. The image drew Li towards itself. Losing his balance Li fell into the depths.

The well was deep and when Li hit the bottom, he had lost all memory as to how he had gotten into this situation. He was stuck and could not figure out what to do. When Cha saw what had happened she leaned over the well and yelled from above. The distance was too great.

Trapped at the bottom of the well, Li began to despair. He could hear nothing but strange echoes. He could see nothing but darkness pricked with a single light. He could feel nothing but water, soil, and stone. After some time, rocks and soil began to fall on him from above. "What evil have I committed to deserve this prison of torment?"

As more rocks and soil fell from above, despair quickly turned to anger. Li began to pace angrily around his hole. When the rocks and soil ceased to fall he would rejoice, when they would continue again he would despair. The cycles continued as Li cursed his lot in life, stomping angrily around his little hole.

Eventually Li noticed something strange, for it seemed that the small prick of light was beginning to grow. Somehow this light in the mist of all the rocks and soil appeared to be getting larger. And yet, when hope would seem to appear, more rocks and soil would begin falling from above.

One day Li heard what sounded like laughing. Anger turned to madness. "What detestable spirit would laugh at such a miserable state?" He stamped and he stomped even harder. Eventually he got so close to the light that he could hear more clearly. From the light above he heard a voice say, "Wake up you silly elephant. It's me your twin Cha. I'm not trying to harm you, I'm trying to help you."

In that moment Li remembered his twin sister and he remembered falling into the well. He realized that his sister was filling the well up with rocks and soil to help him. The rocks and the soil were building a new foundation to lift him higher. With this new realization Li began to stamp and stomp with joy. He now allowed the pain, accepting the rocks and soil with gratitude. Yes they hurt, but it was the pain that was drawing him towards the light.

When Li finally reached the opening, he marveled at what he saw. The sky was bluer than blue. The trees danced like he had never seen them dance. The sun shimmered with glee through each and every leaf. The grass whispered at his feet, and the birds sang songs he had never noticed before. His twin embraced him, and the warmth and love that he felt was beyond measure.

Maypop
The Indescribable

Oh child, do not despair. We are here, and we have never left. We are always speaking, but you are not always listening. We care for each and every part of this great whole. We care for you. Come close little child, for we know why you despair – you have simply forgotten.

> *The way that can be weighed is the solidifying way.*

Why do you still look for something solid? What is solid embodies the process of forgetting, what is flowing embodies the process of remembering. What you so desperately search for, is here now, but it is always moving, always transforming, always transmuting through an unlimited bubbling of forms. It is process, and process can never be directly examined. Halt it and you do not have it.

Structure is a playful illusion, there is only flow.

Love cannot be captured, because Love is a process. How could we make it still? It is not possible. Take the name Maypop that you have clothed us with as an example. Maypop is a word that points to our particular patterning that Love is doing at this particular point within process. As we explore our potential, we are adding to the whole in our own distinctive way. The word Maypop is not who we are. It is a solidifying thing that is pointing to the ongoing process that we are. A name is just a name, but if it points well, it can serve as a temporary guide. In the same way Love has many pointing names. It contains all names, and yet, it is more than every name.

How does the answer find the answer?

Look at your eye. Well, you cannot technically see your eye without the aid of something that reflects. If you wanted to look at your eye, you would need the help of a mirror. What you see in the mirror is not your eye, but a reflection of your eye. The reflection is of a moving eye, an eye that is not still, nor fixed within its environment. The purpose of a mirror is to reflect. If you wish to capture and still the eye in the mirror, you cannot. That is simply something that cannot be done. Yes, you could take a picture of it, but you still have not captured the eye. What you are seeing in the mirror is process, an eye in the process of seeing, and that process is looking back at itself. Love is the universal eye, the spiritual eye, the human eye, the animal eye, the plant eye, the material eye, the atom eye. We are all process, caught up in being and becoming.

Do you wish to truly know Love? Then free it from its captivity. Let go of your cherished preconceptions, topple your graven images of words. Allow the garments of Love to do what they have always been doing – moving you, the process, further along on the great spiral of life.

Look deeply into us and you will see it – unlimited potential, entranced by the play of movement.

Would you like to observe the observer? Look at a leaf as it dances in the wind. Sit upon a mountain and feel its might beneath you. Listen to the sacred songs of the forest. Gaze upon the splendor of the night sky. Watch your lover as they captivate your eye. Feel the touch of your child as they twirl about you. Smell the pure breath of a newborn baby. But also, feel the immense pain of innocence destroyed. Shutter at the compounding torture of nature. Listen to the voice of a dying friend. Smell the rotting flesh of an apple. Walk upon the sleeping roads of winter.

I do not desire, because I am desire. I do not create, because I am creation. I do not exist, because I am existence. I am being because I am becoming.

Love is being in the process of becoming. It is the only way Love can be. Being needs becoming, as light needs darkness. Love as being is unchanging, formless, ever present, and beyond description. And yet its essence is inseparable from its manifestation. Being is light. It is everywhere and yet completely invisible unless there is something to impede itself. The reality and usefulness of light requires reflection in the same way that the reality and usefulness of electricity requires resistance. Impediments and reflection are the process of making the light and the darkness visible, they are the unfolding actualization of infinite potential.

Distance makes the heart grow fonder.

Love, the toroidal clock. Cosmic dawn, a release from an unfathomably still center. Love is on the move. Expansion. Out we go, forcing every force, running, preparing gifts, until all of our outward movements have been exhausted. Pause and reflect. Contraction. Cosmic day, a call to the sleeper, it is time to return home. In we go, remembering and gathering gifts with every step we take. Pause and reflect. Cosmic night, a reunion of process, nothing left to witness, all gifts have been given and received, no separated I, only Am. Unspeakable, unthinkable, indescribable, the dreamless bliss of sleep. We speak of it only from within becoming.

The wise speak of formless God. The playful speak of formed God.

What dreams may come after a dreamless bliss. New adventures, new experiences, exploration through every way imaginable. Expansion, a new cosmic dawn, a new re-imagining, fractaling into process, in-forming itself through realized potential. This is not just a human process, it is an everything process.

In and out, goes the breath of life. In and out, goes the blood of life. In and out, goes the cycles of life.

We are the whole, we are a member, take us into your body and we will help you remember. Creation is creativity in the midst of play, spend time with us and we will help you on your way.

Passiflora spp., Maypop, and Granadilla are a few of our many names. We are many things to many growing things. To you we will become a gift. We offer to you our flowers as a powerful medicine. Learn from the Bumble Bee and lose yourself in them. We offer to you our leaves, fruit, and seeds, all perfectly edible.

Blind Men

Several blind men where sitting together when an enormous elephant was brought into town. None of the blind men had ever heard of an elephant before. Hearing and feeling the loud footsteps they immediately went to investigate.

The first blind man reached out and felt the tail of the elephant. "Surely this great being is like a mighty rope that sways in the wind." The second blind man reached out and felt the leg. "No, it is not like a rope. It is thick and solid, like the trunk of a tree." The third blind man reached out and felt the belly of the elephant. "You all are mistaken. It is large and round, like a giant rock, yet it is rough and pliable." The last blind man reached out and felt the trunk. "I do not know what you three are feeling, but surely this is no rope, trunk, or large rock. It moves and feels like a python, and air passes through its center." The blind men began to argue among themselves.

An intellectual was observing all that was taking place, and laughed. "These poor individuals have no idea what an elephant really is. It is clearly a single plant eating mammal that roams the vast plains and forests of earth." A biologist was sitting nearby and said, "Oh, it is not a single entity. That elephant contains multitudes. It is a universe of microscopic life that we perceive as one entity." A quantum physicist heard the conversation and added, "That animal before you is a dance of movement. It is pure energy. A complex interplay of atoms and subatomic particles/waves." A mystic walked by and proclaimed, "Pure illusion. A beautiful and necessary part of this dream that we call reality."

Finally, a child walked up and upon seeing the mighty elephant fell silent in awe and wonder.

Hopniss
Humility

Oh child, do not despair. We are here, and we have never left. We are always speaking, but you are not always listening. We care for each and every part of this great whole. We care for you. Come close little child, for we know why you despair – you have simply forgotten.

The closer process gets to silence, the more it is silent.

We have watched you sitting along the banks of this great stream. In solitude and emptiness you have discovered us. The ancestors also knew of us, because they too were remembering. We are a reflection of a mysterious whole, cycles of darkness and cycles of light. We bend and we break, we grow and we heal. We contract in the fall, we expand in the spring. We feel both the cold of winter and the warmth of summer.

> *Is there a growing quality in your being? Then there is a growing movement in your understanding.*

You do not yet remember your previous cycles. Forgetting is part of the process. Remembering is too. You have come to the bank of this great stream because you find yourself within the cycle of growing. You are that part of process that is moving from sound into silence. Process takes time.

> *A hand that is always clenched and a hand that is always open are both equally deformed.*

To become the part of process that is returning, humility must take up residence in the heart. Cling only to what you know and you will be like a bird afraid to leave its nest. It is the nature of a bird to fly into the unknown, but, in order to fly, it must first come to the edge of what it knows and let go. Eventually it will need to land again.

> *If I am limited to your understanding, I will only be as big as your understanding.*

Proof? There is no proof that we can offer. Measurements and descriptions of the unknown are not the goal. Being in a state as to be able to receive the unknown, now that is a worthy goal. The intellect can take you far. Humility can take you farther.

Perspective grows when relationships grow.

Learning is a process. It is like learning the alphabet of a higher life. It takes time and much patience to learn these letters. Words and sentences will come in their time. Eventually the ongoing story of Love will be read and lived with clarity and perspective.

> *If I do not exceed your ability to love, then I am not worthy of your love. If I do not exceed your intellect, then I am not worthy of your intelligence. If I am not more reasonable than your highest reasoning, then there is no reason for this.*

If you wish to understand surface things, then isolate, dismember, and dissect us. You will certainly obtain measurements and facts by doing so, but only of the solidifying and not of the flowing. A process cannot be fully understood by attempting to halt or reduce it. The whole is revealed by interacting with it, being in relation to it. This is presence. Reduce an instrument to only its mechanics, and you will miss the purpose of the instrument. Understanding moves with process. To know us, spend time with us. Sit next to us and allow the mystery of Love to speak.

> *When mystery fills your cup, drink it, and return it to emptiness. Only an empty cup is prepared to receive something new.*

What you think you know, is what prevents you from moving forward. Ears no longer listen when ears are full. And yet, ears become full as a reminder that their purpose is to listen. There is no wrong road that could ever be taken. Wrong roads in their time will always reveal the right ones. Going out needs going in, as going in needs going out. Everything is exactly where it should be, learning what needs to be learned, and forgetting what needs to be forgotten. Be patient with process. Allow parts to be becoming in their own way, for each part is already in the hands of the greatest teacher. What need is there to argue and debate, to preach and to pontificate?

Everything is as it should be.

We have been learning for many cycles. We have learned by doing, and in doing we have made plenty of mistakes. Mistakes are our crowning joy. We grow because we have made mistakes. We could not grow if we did not make mistakes. In this we have learned harmony through chaos, balance through imbalance, wholeness through partness, and growth through decay. Continual transformation. In everything lies this pointing.

The flow of a river will find its course. What comes next, is what will come next. Let go of your desire to control it and enjoy its calm and churning waters.

What has been lifted for you is but a tiny corner of a veil. The beauty of the whole is vast and beyond any pointing. To limit sight to only what the separated mind can see, is to remain unaware of the infinite spectrum of seeing. Deep humility allows for the lifting of veils.

Secrets uncovered. Secrets covered. Hide and seek.

We are the whole, we are a member, take us into your body and we will help you remember. Creation is creativity in the midst of play, spend time with us and we will help you on your way.

Apios Americana, Hopniss, Indian Potato, and the American Groundnut are a few of our many names. We are many things to many growing things. To you we will become a gift. We offer to you our flowers as truly stunning edible works of art. We offer to you our tubers as an important source of food. These tubers are at their finest when cooked slowly.

Trapped Monkey

A teacher once took her students to an opening in the forest where many wild monkeys lived. In the middle of this opening was a tree with a small hollow cavity in its trunk. Inside this opening the teacher carefully placed a hard piece of candy.

The monkeys having noticed the candy, quickly made their way to the tree. They pushed and jostled each other, until a large monkey having conquered the others approached and extended its open hand through the hole. It grasped the treasure, but was unable to pull it out with a clinched fist. Frustrated it began to screech.

The students watched as a leopard, having heard the commotion, slowly approached. They yelled at the monkey to run, but the monkey would not let go of what it had attained. The leopard ate the monkey.

The teacher turned to the students and asked, "What killed the monkey?"

Autumn Olive
Clothing and Unclothing

Oh child, do not despair. We are here, and we have never left. We are always speaking, but you are not always listening. We care for each and every part of this great whole. We care for you. Come close little child, for we know why you despair – you have simply forgotten.

Creating an experience. Experiencing a creation.

You have noticed our leaf. Green on one side, silver on the other. Is that all you see? Look closer and you will discover a symphony of nested songs. What you hold in your hand is a song, a culmination of lessons learned and applied. What you see is the beautiful clothing we have put on top of the mystery. It is our story that we created, a story that is now being experienced through you.

One playing with the Many.

Every part of this marvelous universe is caught up in the process of creating something new. We take movements and pattern these into new relationships. We construct relationships and deconstruct relationships. We clothe the mystery and unclothe the mystery. Do not be mistaken, it is not wrong to clothe the mystery. In fact, that is part of the fun. Clothing and unclothing.

Observe our beautiful patterns and you will be observing what relationships can do.

Sometimes we get so caught up in our creations that we forget what we are doing. In adding something new to the mystery we forget to remove the old clothes. We begin layering creative stories on top of older stories. In time the naked mystery becomes heavy with cloth. Garments concealing garments. If these garments are not examined and removed periodically, then they will eventually begin to deteriorate and smell, naturally drawing our attention to themselves.

Garments help us forget. Garments help us remember.

When we start paying attention to these garments, we will examine them and inevitably remove them, layer by layer. When the mystery of being is finally uncovered in all its glory, and its wholeness is on full display, that state is not enduring, and nor do we want it to be. After the ecstasy of union, we will clothe ourselves again. Love in all its glory, for it to be Love, necessitates clothing. Being in all its glory, for it to be being, necessitates becoming. And consciously creating the garments of Love, is an exciting and exhilarating part of the process. This is the game of balance. Sometimes we play the hiding part, sometimes we play the seeking part, but we are always playing, always patterning, always creating.

> *How are you clothing? Have you noticed the garments you have placed over Love? Are they thick and layered, worn and withered, stained and full of stench?*

A flexible story will flow with every situation. The lightest stories, like the lightest garments, are not rigid, they move and flow, grow and evolve. They are constructed with awareness and knowledge of their impermanence. They are open to alteration and revision. And yet even the wisest craftsman becomes intoxicated by beauty.

Beautiful garments give birth to more beautiful garments until we are again taken in by our own artistry and forget what we are doing. Entranced by the power of creativity, we will continue the cycles and obscure the light beneath. With our mind on garments, we will add layer upon layer to the mystery, stories will give birth to new stories, light and flowing stories will eventually become layered with heavy and rigid ones. Darkness will cast its shadow. We will lose sight of the mystery that hides beneath. Play will be playing us again. That is the nature of play.

Voluntary hypnosis.

Garments should not be despised, as they are the very guides that lead us back to reunion. When garments are continually worn, they will start to wear out. Holes will appear, threads will loosen, and colors will gray. A part that was distracted, will start to pay attention. It is separation that makes reunion possible. It is separation as well as reunion to which we pledge our allegiance. Movement goes both ways.

> *We paint a picture in the mind – light brush strokes of semi-transparent paint. When our painting is understood, either throw the picture away, or add new layers to it.*

We are the whole, we are a member, take us into your body and we will help you remember. Creation is creativity in the midst of play, spend time with us and we will help you on your way.

Elaeagnus spp., Autumn Olive, and Goumi are a few of our many names. We are many things to many growing things. To you we will become a gift. We offer to you our flesh as portals to unseen perspective. Combine us with care. We offer to you our fruit and our seeds, all perfectly edible.

Power of Maya

Narada was a lover of God who prayed and meditated with fervor each day. One day God appeared to Narada and promised to grant him anything that he wished. Narada thought for a moment and then responded, "I wish to understand the power of your Maya."

God agreed to show Narada the power of Maya, but first asked Narada to take a walk with him. Narada found himself walking with God upon the rolling hills of a hot desert terrain. God, feeling thirsty, pointed Narada to a village off in the distance and asked him to bring back some water.

Narada went to the village and knocked at the door of the first house he could find. A beautiful young woman opened the door and upon seeing her, Narada became mesmerized and completely forgot why he had come to the house. The young woman invited him in and he was received by her family with great joy. Narada was intoxicated with love.

Narada eventually married the lovely young woman and after five years had three beautiful children. The family moved into a small village hut and lived a very humble life, experiencing both joys and hardships.

One day an incredibly fierce storm hit their village. As the waters began to rise Narada took his wife and three children and made their way towards higher ground. As he struggled to get through the rising water, he stumbled and fell. The two smallest children slipped from his hands and were swept away by the water. Narada tried to swim after them, but it was too late, the current had swept them away. As he looked back at his wife and child, he watched helplessly as the water suddenly rose up and swallowed them too.

Narada swam over to a large rock and collapsed. Replaying all his misfortune he wept with the bitterest of tears. Suddenly he heard what sounded like a familiar voice. "My child. Where is the water that you were supposed to bring me? I have been waiting patiently for almost an hour." Narada turned his head towards the voice and instead of an all-consuming flood, he found himself stretched out on the hot desert terrain.

Taking his hand God asked, "Now do you understand the power of our Maya?"

Mushroom
A Big Act

Oh child, do not despair. We are here, and we have never left. We are always speaking, but you are not always listening. We care for each and every part of this great whole. We care for you. Come close little child, for we know why you despair – you have simply forgotten.

> *If linear mind wants to know, linear mind must learn to bend. It is the spiraling mind that sees itself.*

Why do you cast fear aside and enter the dark caves? Why do you seek the silent places? Why do you touch what you are told not to touch? Yes, you are starting to remember.

There is really nothing to fear.

Life is a story, a growing, developing, layering sort of thing. Stories are always combining, rearranging, reinventing and fashioning themselves into something new. A story may be made up of words, but words are only the pointers. The movement that make stories real are words dramatized, imagined, invoked, and actualized. Stories include the actors, the audience, and the stage upon which the drama plays out. Stories are all of us, the fractaling eyes that see and the fractaling eyes that are seen. The being and the becoming. The actors, the audience, the stage, and the drama.

Go to the trees, they have much to share.

Our nature is to dream, it is what we do. Giving birth to dreams within dreams within solid dreams. The creative alchemy of play. Be still and remember. With every in breath and out breath, throughout each expansion and contraction, we have been creating newer and more exciting plays and ways to play. It is what you do when you can do anything.

> *Observe the child, not far removed from the mystery. Remembering, she plays: laughter and peek-a-boo, adventures and magic, stories and dramas, hide and go seek, art and form, pretend and laughter.*

When we started this cycle, we knew it was play, as every audience knows before an act begins. We dreamed, storied, and patterned together. We worked on becoming the stage, the props, and the settings. We invented, built, shaped, and fabricated, setting the stage for a new and exciting act.

We knew intimately the mechanics of this act, but what we didn't know was the journey, the experience of being completely taken in by the act. An audience would not be captivated by a magician that allowed the mechanics of a trick to be known. A performance would lack imagination if the actors had rigid lines. Therefore, some parts hid so that other parts could seek. Those that entered into this drama as both actor and audience naturally became captivated by it. The performance draws us in and compels us to forget. Veils hide what would ruin the play if seen. We play and then we become intoxicated with playing.

> *I have drunken from the vine of my own artistry. I have forgotten the way home. All is well.*

A good act must have perceivable boundaries. The stage must maintain certain limitations if it is to be believable. As more and more points of awareness lose themselves into their ever expanding roles, a most convincing illusion of reality appears. The audience and actors cannot remember why they did this. Enchantment sets in. The spell of creativity binds us. And this is where the play really takes off, for the depths of the illusion take the drama beyond what a lineated mind can comprehend. In forgetting who and what we are, the play is able to actualize and explore new heights and new depths, new light and new darkness.

> *Do not fear, for everything is as it should be. Forms will come and go, like limbs dancing beneath a sheet. Do not fear, for I have sent you nothing but myself.*

Realization takes time, like a tree that slowly adds to itself, always stretching into something new. It is a process, and this process can be terrifying when it is not seen with perspective. The play will drag you around, it will push you down, abusing and insulting you. And you will take it seriously. So seriously in fact, that you will drag others around, you will push them down, abusing and insulting them. And they will take it seriously. This is what makes the play so interesting. Mystery clothing itself with infinite forms, pretending not to be itself. Love dancing with chaos and order.

If your path is moving out of chaos, you will start creating new ways of relating, using these relationships to bring forth those qualities of light. If your path is moving out of order, you will start creating new ways of separating, using separation to bring forth those qualities of darkness. The world is not either/or. It is both/and.

Process has a purpose. Process is the purpose.

Conceptually, it is an easy thing to realize that the world is a stage, and this particular you is both actor and audience. What now? Do you drop out of the play? Impossible! For there is only play. What remains is to do the hard thing – to be the part of the mystery that is forgiving, compassionate, loving, kind, peaceful, and joyful. The acting does not end. Instead the actor acts with a growing awareness and realization. This is the part of the play where we can really laugh at our roles and our masks.

Why take offense when a blind man strikes you?

When actualization starts on this new level, actors begin the process of creating and developing a new story. It is improvisation accompanied by awareness. It is spontaneity accompanied by perspective. With a hidden wink and a nod, the other is silently thanked for providing the most wonderful gift of experience. The show will go on because that is its nature. The actor will then marvel at creation, being overwhelmed with a deep sense of gratitude and awe, for that is its nature. We become children again, close to source, able to see the magic contained within everything – laughter and peek-a-boo, adventures and magic, stories and dramas, hide and go seek, art and form, pretend and laughter. We live, die, and live again, infinite eyes to see infinity. Becoming. Being. Becoming again.

Gratitude! Unspeakable gratitude!

Life is serious business, because that is the power given to it. A problem is only a problem when the mind believes there is a problem. Take that power away and life becomes a marvelous game. Any game worth playing, should not be easy. For if it is not capable of capturing our attention, we would never have started playing it.

Good and bad will still chase each other, and you too will pretend to chase them, but with full knowledge that good vs. evil makes for a most captivating and educational drama. The drama like all good music will have its ups and downs, its pauses and its rests. It will play with the discord, and release its tension through harmony. There will be joy and there will be sorrow, there will be winning and there will be losing.

> *Enlightenment is not simply to understand, it is to marvel.*

We are the whole, we are a member, take us into your body and we will help you remember. Creation is creativity in the midst of play, spend time with us and we will help you on your way.

We will not give you what you want. You are a we, and we know what we need. We are here for your benefit. We are here for your detriment. A mushroom can be both a destructive poison and at the same time a healing medicine. Destroy you or grow you? Perhaps we will do both.

We are not here so that you can escape reality. We are here to help you remember reality. Take us lightly and we will show you heaviness. We are a chemical lock, and if the key fits, we will momentarily free you from habitual ways of thinking. We put us here, like sacred gems hidden within the sacred rocks. The dark cave must be entered before the treasure can be found.

When fear has been surrendered, we will write upon your mind. Our writing is so dangerous to the linear mind that it is often illegal. And that too is a necessary part of the drama. Slaves who are not ready, will sit at their master's feet. Those who understand freedom, no longer need to sit at their teacher's feet.

Cling to us and you will know peril. A sign post is not a sitting post. It is the fool in his folly who is satisfied with pointings. It is the wise in his wisdom who thanks the sign post, leaves it behind, and then plans the next route accordingly.

Hidden in Plain Sight

There once lived a very inquisitive man named Icarus, who found himself born into a labyrinth of questions. Since birth he had been perplexed by his and everyone else's existence. He would be amazed by his hands, the symmetry, the movement, the colors, and ask; "Why should they exist at all? Why should anything exist out of nothingness?" Life for Icarus was the greatest miracle of all, but his mind could not comprehend it.

In search of answers he first started to build wings out of ideas that he had inherited. These were familial and communal ideas, and these absolutely worked. He could fly. But there was a catch. Icarus was told that these wings had limitations, that there were some questions that could not be asked, and some places where the wings would not work. Ignoring the limitations, Icarus flew with certainty, and drawn by the light of the sun, he flew high. But his wings were made of wax, and quickly melted. He fell into the sea and eventually washed up onto a labyrinth of more questions.

Filled with despair, he pulled off the broken fragments of his inherited ideas and began to study. He separated himself from nature and began to observe it through a lens. His observations and his studies led to theories, and these theories led to new ideas, testable ideas. He reduced these ideas into standard and definable parts, and with these parts he started to build new wings. These ideas worked. Icarus could fly. Drawn again by the light of the sun, he headed towards it with certainty. But his wings suffered a Gödelian incompleteness, being made of steel, they quickly melted away. He again fell into the sea and eventually washed up onto a labyrinth of questions.

Filled with despair, he pulled off the empty fabrications of knowledge and concepts that were clinging to him. It was in this moment that he cried – and let go. His mind surrendered, and his heart humbly affirmed, "We are ready." Slowly his eyes started to open, and he began to see what he could not see before – the living hieroglyphs of the natural world that were moving all around him and through him. He laughed and then he wept.

Mulberry

Connection

Oh child, do not despair. We are here, and we have never left. We are always speaking, but you are not always listening. We care for each and every part of this great whole. We care for you. Come close little child, for we know why you despair – you have simply forgotten.

Love, the beautiful Mother of ten thousand things.

Can you see the clouds floating in our leaves? Do you see the sun moving through our branches? Can you feel the wind that moves within our trunk? Can you hear the animals that have become our feet? Have you noticed the eyes that have become our eyes?

Nothing exists unless it is in relation to something else. There is an interdependence between poles, as one invokes the other. The universe is becoming what it is becoming through the interdependence of movement. It is a cooperating process that unfolds itself through playing with competition. This is how Love is able to see itself.

We are considered to be a whole tree, but our whole is made up of many cooperating and competing parts. Each part of us is dependent upon every other part. Competition teaches us and makes our parts strong, while cooperation connects these parts into larger wholes.

Leaves need branches and branches need leaves. Roots need leaves and leaves need roots. Trunks need roots and roots need trunks. But it does not stop with the tree. Trees need the galaxies, suns, moons, solar winds, clouds, rain, soil, rocks, insects, worms, animals, fungi, bacteria, eyes, etc. The list is unending as it contains every movement.

We are the big moving whole. We are not separate from it, we are simply different aspects of it. The big moving whole is made up of parts, which have their own unique wholeness, that are themselves made up of smaller parts. Go up or go down, and you will find wholes dependent upon parts and parts dependent upon wholes.

Observe the connection between your lungs and the universe. Lungs are very much a part of you. But what are lungs without air. If air does not flow through your lungs, then there are no lungs. Air is as much a part of you as your lungs are. But what is air without plants? Plants are as much a part of you as air and lungs are. And what are plants without an atmosphere? The atmosphere is as much a part of you as plants, air, and lungs are.

Self is not limited to the part that is contained within the skin. Just as the body is the lungs, it is also the suns, moons, clouds, wind, rain, soil, rocks, insects, animals, fungi, bacteria, eyes, etc. The list is infinite. Everything is a vital extension of a larger self. At each level, process fractals, and every fractal is both separate and interdependent. The universe requires separate and yet interdependent parts for it to be. Lungs need air, galaxies need atoms, and hate needs forgiveness.

The process of becoming is flowing like a river, and that river not only runs through you, it is you. As eyes become whole they begin seeing how separation plays with interdependence. Air and lungs, insects and flowers, laughing and crying, competition and cooperation, peace and war, offense and forgiveness – what Love is doing in this moment. Everything is Love caught up in movement, dancing the dance of life. It is what Love does.

Re-union is re-membering. As the dis-membered parts are re-membered to be one big connected whole, we begin seeing more clearly the one dancing under the disguise of multiplicity.

When parts start to remember, they know that what is done to other parts is truly done to themselves, and what they hate in other parts is what they hate in themselves.

Love thy other, and you will love thyself.

We are the whole, we are a member, take us into your body and we will help you remember. Creation is creativity in the midst of play, spend time with us and we will help you on your way.

Morus spp., and Mulberry are a few of our many names. We are many things to many growing things. To you we will become a gift. We offer to you our fruit in abundance. When the time is right, spread a sheet beneath our branches and shake. Like manna from heaven, we will rain down gifts.

Parts on Strike

One day the feet decided to go on strike against the stomach. "We carry you back and forth, up and down, over and under, all so you can eat. We are calloused, sore, and tired. What do we get in return? Nothing. You just sit there day after day. We are done working."

The hands then decided to join in on the strike. "We are in agreement with the feet. Each day we hammer and nail, push and pull, lift and drop, all so you can eat. What do we get in return? Nothing. You just sit there day after day. We are also done working."

The mouth then decided to join in on the strike. "I am also done working. I chew and chew, and then I chew some more, all so you can eat. What do I get in return? Nothing. You just sit there day after day."

After many days of doing nothing, the feet realized that they were having trouble walking. The hands noticed that they could barely move. The mouth pondered why it was so dry and sticky. After a quick meeting they decided to ask the heart.

"Foolishness is a wonderful teacher," said the heart. "Though the stomach may be silent, though it cannot be seen, it has been working tirelessly in its own quiet way. We are all connected. We are one body that contains many different and unique parts. If parts go on strike, the whole will become a wonderful teacher."

The feet, hands, and the mouth all agreed that they were gravely mistaken. After a quick apology to the whole, they got back to work.

Serviceberry
Music of Being and Becoming

Oh child, do not despair. We are here, and we have never left. We are always speaking, but you are not always listening. We care for each and every part of this great whole. We care for you. Come close little child, for we know why you despair – you have simply forgotten.

Trust

Music is a pattern of vibrating relationships. Taste our fruit. That is not a static chemical substance you taste. It is music – the patterning structure of our creative nature. Our geometry is beautiful, because we have grown into beauty.

Music is built on relationships. It is constructed not only through the harmonic intervals that exist between notes, but also through the resolution of discordant notes. When combinations of notes relate and resolve well, beautiful music is created.

The music that is the universe operates the same way. It is not something that exists without dissonance, rather it is something that understands the purpose of dissonance. Dissonance makes things interesting by way of resolution. The world is not simply in conflict with its opposite, rather, they are playing, like poles that give tension to a musical string. It is the tension and interplay of opposing forces that makes harmony possible.

Listen to discordant notes and you will feel an inward pull towards that which resolves the tension.

Life is the interplay of opposites and it provides us with innumerable strings from which to play. A note that is played well is not trying to be victorious in the struggle of opposing poles, a growing note accepts the necessary tension and adjusts itself accordingly until balance is discovered. A note by itself is mildly interesting, but what makes a note more interesting is how it relates to other notes. What is their relationship? A growing movement of awareness can not help but ask, "Is it beautiful?"

A note by itself is neither true or false, right or wrong. It is the movement of multiple notes in relation to each other that produces something interesting. This process brings discord and harmony into focus. Love is movement and movement is the complex interplaying of notes. How notes relate determine what type of music is being played.

There are songs of freedom and there are songs of captivity and there is everything in between.

When the music of the universe is on its upward swing, it is the resolution of discordant notes that draw out beauty. When the dissonance of hatred is resolved by the chords of forgiveness – that is interesting, that is beautiful. When the chaos of war is transmuted into the tranquility of peace – that is interesting, that is beautiful. When the heaviness of discontentment is transformed into the notes of contentment – that is interesting, that is beautiful. When the terror of despair is replaced with the harmony of trust – that is interesting, that is beautiful.

Discernment tells us that God is unspeakable light. Acceptance tells us that God is unspeakable darkness.

Life is often tragic, leading through some of the darkest nights, but it is the discord that paves the way for harmony. It is discord that draws out new color and depth. Uplifting music is not a blissful state of pure perfection, rather it is music being won at every moment from the hands of tragedy.

Pain, abuse, suffering, and torture, these are the terrifying shadows that remind us of the light. They are the alchemical ingredients from which beauty can be distilled. Though they can be incredibly dark and disturbing, they are a necessary part of the richness and depth that is the music of the universe.

Climb up to beauty by way of pain. Climb down to pain by way of beauty.

The purpose of music is not to get to the end of the song as fast as possible. Every song has its beginning and its end, but those are necessary parts within a larger process. Music exists to be experienced, played, and enjoyed. Life is the process of creating new songs, new worlds, new ways of seeing, and new ways of becoming. Our very being is the eternal and unceasing music of life.

You are a human instrument, but that is not the only instrument. The human instrument is one particular tool to experience and express process. The human instrument is one among a multitude of instruments. With every cycle instruments add to the process in their own unique ways.

Our plant instruments are not separate from this process, but rather are vital to it. Every instrument takes discordant relationships and transmutes them. Tension in whatever form it takes carries with it the potential to create notes that can exist in harmonious relationships. When harmonious notes are discovered and resolution is found, it creates a sound that resonates throughout the entire spectrum. Music ripples through reality, affecting other instruments all the way down and back up again. Enlightenment playing with chaos. Chaos playing with enlightenment.

Do not preach. Merely be an example of what harmony can do.

We are the whole, we are a member, take us into your body and we will help you remember. Creation is creativity in the midst of play, spend time with us and we will help you on your way.

Amelanchier spp., Saskatoon, Juneberry, and Serviceberry are a few of our many names. We are many things to many growing things. To you we will become a gift. We offer to you our fruit as something beyond words.

Tzu and the Great Hall

Within the Great Hall of Actualization, a newly crafted piano begins to fade into view. Beautifully assembled for perfection and imperfection. Eighty eight keys of potential sound, contained within seven octaves. Limits for the concentration of experience. Tzu once again sits at the piano.

The Great Hall is beginning to fill. Angelic rays of golden light are flowing about, filling the empty spaces. Eyes are everywhere – witnessing, watching, savoring. Oh, how they love to watch the great waves of discord begin their upsurge into music. They have been here before.

They have watched Tzu many times pounding her keys, filling the space around her with dissonance. Dissonance breeds. It is what dissonance does. Pain, strife, jealousy, anger, resentment, selfishness, hatred, confusion, sadness. Tzu victimizing Tzu.

Yet within this moment of process, something is different. There is a stirring in the hall, a movement of feeling, a whispering of harmony. The Great Hall of Actualization is once again pulsating with the energy of anticipation. Only the long and intense labor of time could produce such an electrifying atmosphere. The watchers are Tzu and Tzu is all of them.

A hush comes over the hall as Tzu appears on the stage. She is seated awkwardly in front of her piano. Above her the dissonance begins to circle, swirling waves of sound, moving uncomfortably through the air. Dissonance is an honored guest, and upon its entrance, the great hall of watchers bow in silent reverence. Regardless of how dark and deformed the waves have become, they are seen as the bringers of harmony, necessary and revered teachers.

Fixated on Tzu, the eyes witness a subtle change that begins to come over her. She no longer is pounding her keys but is now sitting in silence. She shifts and moves uncomfortably, as if trying to feel the purpose behind the discomfort. She turns her head slightly, attuning her ear to a new sound that lies hidden within the dissonance. A hushed smattering of whispers echoes throughout the great hall, "She hears it! She is remembering!" Oh, the excitement of anticipation. Tzu, is remembering, and the eyes that are watching know it. The great ascent is beginning.

The discord has brought her to an encounter with the song of being and becoming – the Love upon which everything rests. She has heard the purpose and the purpose has heard her. The process of her transformation has reached its turning point. Tzu sits in silence, no longer despairing within the labyrinth of dissonance. Silence has been felt within the noise. Noise has been felt within the silence. After a long period of listening and learning, Tzu begins to play her instrument again.

At first it is a note here and then a note there. These relate well, and so she adds more. With each passing cycle, she begins to add more notes, and these eventually turn into chords. Soon harmonies are harmonizing, and new melodies are being played on top. Oh, the sweet sound of growth!

Tzu now accepts the waves of dissonance, and actively feeds them into her piano. Dissonance becomes transformed into the most beautiful waves of interrelating tones. Harmonies now merge with new harmonies. Unrealized melodies come into being.

As the last waves of dissonance transform into hidden waves of light, the music takes over. It merges and becomes Tzu. She no longer even tries. Becoming moves into Being. The great Performer once again realizes that she is the Performance. This is the musical alchemy of the universe. This is the purpose of actualization. This is what the watchers have been witnessing all along. This is eternal return.

Tzu has become light by becoming light. With nothing to weigh her down, she ascends. She surrenders her name. She surrenders her human instrument. And with an explosion of light, the waves of music become so bright that she is transformed into the mystery of Being.

Drawn in, only to be drawn out again.

Wild Rose
Seed of Being

Oh child, do not despair. We are here, and we have never left. We are always speaking, but you are not always listening. We care for each and every part of this great whole. We care for you. Come close little child, for we know why you despair – you have simply forgotten.

Love alone is worth the struggle.

Observe our forms. We grow and we decay. It is the law of our being. As we grow, we change, transforming matter into new matter. Our nature carries us from seed to seed. We are birthed out of seed, we explore, we struggle, and then we journey back into seed.

But it is not the same seed, it is a changed seed. The journey into a new seed is what changes the next seed.

The mechanics of the game are known. The journey through the game, being gamed by the game – that is the intoxicating unknown.

To begin an upward movement requires a lower order. We've all been to those depths. In that state we did not know exactly what the higher order was doing. We could not see it or comprehend it. We were limited for a reason. What is the point of being overwhelmed with more than we were capable of understanding? It would take all the fun out of the game.

Cloud unknowing.

The sun, soil, wind, and rain, appeared to us as terrible threats. It is our nature to grow and so we grew, we learned that the darkness of the soil was needed as much as the light of the sun. We learned that the wind was just as important to making us strong as the rain was. We learned to direct energy away from branches that grew into dark places. We learned to let go of old ways of searching for light, so that new ways could climb higher.

Seeds are Love exploring itself.

Process allows us to learn how to play within our material environments. From seed to seed, we did the best we could. The outcome was unknown, but we did not worry about it. We knew it was worth the sacrifice, or else we would not be here. So we did the only thing that we could do – we moved. Movement is what allowed us to learn. When we were capable of seeing with new eyes the little spot we inhabited, our perspective eventually expanded to a larger spot. We have all come far. Our growing and decaying forms are an important story of what Love creates.

Deep within a seed, written upon the unseen,
lies a luminous record.

The purpose of life is to live. And to live is to grow and decay. With every cycle our little seed is thrown into inconceivable worlds, reflections of the acquired wealth of the whole. What is needed to grow within this new world is already contained within. Our cycle of decay has brought us back to growth, the new seed has sprouted from the old. Growth is underway, gifts are being given back to the whole. The wind and the rain are transforming us into growing beauty. The soil and the sun are pushing us into new heights. It is happening without any unnecessary force. It is process, and process is always unfolding.

The force that is forced is not the growing force.

Growth is another word for play. It is our nature to play. We have never stopped playing, we only forgot that we were playing. The point of playing is also growth. You would not play a game if you constantly got worse at playing a game. You play and become lost in play, because to truly play is to get caught up in a game. With time you naturally get better at playing, simply because you are playing. With each movement your performance improves, better moves are made, choices are done with increasing awareness, and perspective is gained. It is this process that not only allows our growing part to see, but to see further, love more deeply, absorb more fully, act more patiently, and forgive more quickly. This is lucid playing. The great art of improvisation.

Knowing about a game and playing a game are two very different things.

True play is much like going to sleep. Force yourself to sleep and you will lie in bed awake. Let go and you will fall into sleep. If you try to attain sleep you will lose it. If you let go, sleep will find you. Play is not actively trying to attain something. Its goal is not to get back to seed. It knows that this will occur and if it does not, then that part of play was not meant to make it back to seed. True play is play that serves no particular purpose other than play. Play will always accomplish what it needs to, because it is natural and spontaneous. Place a group of children in a field with no expectations and they will play. It is what we all do.

Love, without expectations.

The particular game that you have been playing is coming to its natural conclusion. Pretending that you are a separated being within a universe that is outside of you is coming to an end. The game is closing one chapter and opening another. This new chapter is playful awareness. It is characterized by fearlessness and wonder, exploration and spontaneity, compassion and awe, creativity and perspective. Where it leads does not matter, because where it ends, what seed is produced, is the exact seed that needed to be produced.

Arrive where you started. Know it for the first time.

The pages of the universe do not turn over night. Love cherishes a long and deep story. It savors every little detail. Growth is process, and nothing can skip process. Growth takes time. This chapter is ending, a new chapter is being glimpsed, but there is no hurry. The page will turn when it is ready to turn.

To rush into the light, is to be blinded by the light.

We are the whole, we are a member, take us into your body and we will help you remember. Creation is creativity in the midst of play, spend time with us and we will help you on your way.

Rosa rugosa, Ramanas Rose, and Rugosa Rose are a few of our many names. We are many things to many growing things. To you we will become a gift. We offer to you our fruits, flowers, and young shoots to eat, all perfectly edible. We offer to you some of our seeds to use as flour.

Sprout Little Seed Sprout

Little seed that has fallen below,
Open your eyes, for it's time to grow.
Whispers are stirring from deep within,
It's time to listen, it's time to begin.

Push up, push down, push left, push right,
Push out of the known, with all your might.
And when you are free, from that comfortable cave,
You must be strong, and you must be brave.

Bumps and bruises, will steer you along,
Bumps and bruises, are life's learning song.
Darkness, uncertainty, and things you can't see,
That is the process of being free.

Push through the darkness that holds you in place,
And before you know it, you will feel its embrace.
Golden color will stream all around,
Light so bright that it will truly astound.

But here is a secret, I tell you it's true,
That light you see, it's only a hue.
Towering giants filter your light,
Towering giants protect your sight.

Now it is quite natural, to think you can bloom,
But you are still fragile, just out of the womb.
Growth is a process that must slowly unfold,
With lessons to learn and lessons to mold.

So welcome those winds that push you over,
And welcome the rains that make you sober.
The wind is a friend that will push you along,
And those beating rains will help you grow strong.

But to grow is something that you must choose,
For the path of decay awaits those who refuse.
So send out your branches every which way,
Reach for the light, it is time to play.

But don't forget, to send your roots deep,
Into the darkness, past those who sleep.
Go deeper and deeper, there is nothing to fear,
Darkness is needed, for light to appear.

Touching the light means finding dark places,
And eventually, you will find some dark spaces.
Leaves will turn yellow, and then a brown red,
So pay close attention, or a sickness may spread.

Learn from this branch, and let it fall clear,
When wrong paths are taken, right ones appear.
Direct your energy to branches with light,
As shadowy places will often bring blight.

Now a time will come when purpose is sought,
"Why am I here?" will consume your thoughts.
"Where do I start, and where do I begin?"
To answer these questions, you must look within.

Labyrinths are created from thinking it through,
But the heart always points, to the union of two.
Light is forever, your beautiful half,
And when you embrace it, you may start to laugh.

You create with light, and light creates with you,
And because of this relationship, you create something new.
Light must be reflected, for its own actuality,
And how you relate to it, will create your reality.

So when seasons come, and seasons go,
What really matters, is the direction of flow.
Did you flow with forgiveness, or did you cling to hate?
Did you destroy or did you create?

Did you cooperate or did you compete?
Were your fruits bitter or were they quite sweet?
How much did you give, how much did you take?
Were you paying attention, were you even awake?

Were rocks and hard soil too much to bear?
Did the wind and rain cause you to despair?
Or did you move through and find realization?
Regardless of your lot, regardless of your station.

If your roots go deep and your branches high,
You will be ready, when your enfoldment draws nigh.
Songs will be sung, as autumn winds blow,
Songs will be sung, in a glorious show.

Masterpiece of colors, created in light,
Beautiful colors, prepare for the night.
And when these colors all start to drain,
You will not mourn, for something remains.

And when all that's left is a tiny little seed,
All that's left is exactly what you need.
It is not dying, but dying into being,
New ways of living, new ways of seeing.

A growing seed, will become one once more,
Thrown back into darkness, made to explore.
Life is not a circle, meant to keep you bound,
Rather life is a spiral, a mystery of sound.

Spirals are circles if seeds refuse to grow,
Spirals are circles when seeds stay below.
So let warmth and water find their way through,
Let warmth and water do what they do.

Sprout little seed, sprout,
It is time to push out.
Sprout little seed, sprout,
For that is what life is all about.

Stinging Nettle
Everything as Master

Oh child, do not despair. We are here, and we have never left. We are always speaking, but you are not always listening. We care for each and every part of this great whole. We care for you. Come close little child, for we know why you despair – you have simply forgotten.

Movement is what moves us.

To be stung by us hurts, and yet, that sting is a great gift, that is, when you understand what a sting is doing. Pain is your teacher, master, and educator. Pleasure is your teacher, master, and educator. Open your eyes and you will see your teacher's outer form. Close your eyes and you will see your teacher's inner form. Movement is teacher, master, and educator.

> *Do not neglect the masters before you. The blade of grass is your master, learn from it. The seed that is carried by the wind is your master, learn from it. The rain that is falling from the sky is your master, learn from it. The trauma you suffered as a child is your master, learn from it. The family you were born into is your master, learn from them. The circumstances of life are your master, learn from them. The thoughts that dance through your mind are your master, learn from them.*

Process is the journey from point, out into the unknown, and then back into changed point. A great never ending torus of spiraling movement. The reality presented to each of us is the teacher, and every experience, circumstance, difficulty, joy, pain, sorrow, and pleasure is teaching. Learning environments transform us into something new.

> *Two choices are currently before you – be the victim or be the student.*

Look around you. The people in your life, are the very people that need to be in your life. The circumstances of your life, are the very circumstances that need to be in your life. The environments that surround your life, are the very environments that need to surround your life. Becoming is not punitive, it is corrective.

> *Greater the hardship, greater the learning.*

Ignore a lesson and it will find you again. The lesson is you and you cannot ignore what you fundamentally are. Lessons only get louder until they capture attention. Force creates counterforce. Push against a stream and it will push back, because that is the direction of its flow. To fight process is to push against flow. Eventually we yield.

I am elastic. Move away from me, and you will feel the pull to return.

Counterforce is what shakes us and asks us to notice. If you are paying attention to the lessons of life you will allow a bad experience to become a wonderful tool for transformation. When lessons have been learned, you will laugh at your previous attempt to force that which cannot be forced. You will see the respective poles and the opportunity that they have created for you. You will be thankful, as the problems of life were the very things that brought about growth. It is only through taking the wrong path that qualities of light are able to emerge.

Do you wish to be molded? Then learn to melt.

Remembering the plan of being does not make negative experiences go away, it only brings awareness to the purpose of negative experiences. Pain is only a punishment if we ignore its purpose. Place your hand in a fire and the fire will teach you of a better way. The fire's nature is to burn. Your hand's nature is not to burn. Love is not punishing you, it is teaching you. Fighting against an effect while preserving the cause is a necessary part of process, but it will only last for a time.

Fortune is dancing with misfortune.

Learning the lessons of life does not mean escape. Awareness does not take us out of a painful world, because where there is no pain there is no pleasure. There will still be sadness, but we will recognize it as a product of knowing joy. There will still be hatred, but we will recognize it as the bringer of forgiveness. There will still be scarcity, because there is plenty. There will be winter, because there is summer. One without the other is incomplete and an impossibility within a whole.

All roads lead to God, because all roads lead away from God.

Pain and suffering create necessary pressure. As pressure increases, movement begins to change. Pain and suffering move us because that is their purpose. Ignorance will always move us towards the pole of pain, which eventually creates enough pressure so as to move us in a different direction. This movement of expanding and contracting is the law of the universe. Unity moves out into Separateness. Pressure builds. Separateness moves back into Unity.

How much greater the morning, when great has been the night.

As in any play, it is the conflict that brings about new novelty, excitement, and new ways of seeing. Resolving the conflict is the part of the play where harmony is found. Creating conflict is the part of the play where dissonance is found. When habits get disrupted, new realities are found. Disruption is master, teacher, educator.

> *What is a play without a performer? What is a performer without a performance? What is a performance without a problem?*

We are the whole, we are a member, take us into your body and we will help you remember. Creation is creativity in the midst of play, spend time with us and we will help you on your way.

Urtica dioica, Nettle, and Stinging Nettle are a few of our many names. We are many things to many growing things. To you we will become a gift. We offer to you our young leaves to eat, all perfectly edible. Dry or cook the leaves if you wish to remove our healing sting.

The Student and Teacher

One evening a teacher was sitting alone while drinking some Nettle tea. A thief with a gun jumped through a window and shouted, "Show me where your money is or I will kill you!"

The teacher unmoved and still sipping on Nettle tea told the thief, "You will find all of my money over there in the drawer." Then he returned to sipping the Nettle tea.

As the thief was getting ready to leave, the teacher called out, "Do not accept it all. I am going to the market tomorrow in order to buy some food." The thief, slightly puzzled, decided to return a small portion of the money.

As he was again getting ready to leave, the teacher added, "It is important to thank a person when you receive a gift." The thief, even more puzzled, thanked him and quickly left.

A few days later, the thief was caught and charged with many crimes. When the great teacher was called as a witness he spoke to the court.

"As far as I can tell, this man is no thief. He did indeed visit my home a few days ago. I gave him money and he even thanked me for it."

The thief immediately wept.

Dandelion
Problems

Oh child, do not despair. We are here, and we have never left. We are always speaking, but you are not always listening. We care for each and every part of this great whole. We care for you. Come close little child, for we know why you despair – you have simply forgotten.

Problems are simply a lack of perspective.

Evil is not a problem to run from. Evil is a teacher to be thanked. If anyone is to be good, then someone must be bad. If joy is to be a possibility, pain must be accepted. A diamond is only seen as a diamond after it has encountered something rough. If light is to be distilled, darkness must be a necessary part of this process.

> *I am the Beautiful and the Good. I reveal myself through evoking that which is not Beautiful and Good.*

Peace, patience, and kindness are good because they are good. We accept the good. War, wickedness, and evil are bad because they are bad. We accept the bad. When we understand darkness as the veiling of light, when we grasp the necessity of bad so that good can be, we accept the bad with gratitude, as a cherished friend and not an enemy.

An enlightened state is any state that understands what movement is doing. Life is not about escaping life. The goal is not to get rid of the I, but rather to expand its circumference. There is no hurry in this. Life is not a race. It is a dance, and this dance is happening now and will continue happening until all movement is exhausted.

> *The wise and the foolish are both servants of Love.*

Changing movement from descending to ascending will often require external forces. External laws, codes, and creeds, are important steps along the journey. Sometimes we need something that appears solid to hold onto. And yet, there will come a time when insight into the nature of things is remembered. External laws, codes, and creeds will fall away, as what is written on the heart will surface. Action will then flow freely with process.

If someone takes your coat, then that coat becomes a gift to the new owner. If someone strikes you on the cheek, an opportunity to be forgiveness is presented. If someone forces you to walk a mile, you will walk two. Your awareness will have enlightened both you and your forgetting part to the mysterious game that is being played.

To be offended is to not be paying attention.

Reality is built for instructive experience. An enemy is never a problem, but an opportunity to play with new qualities. A discordant note is never a problem, but an opportunity to learn better relationships.

When everything is understood, everything is forgiven.

We are the whole, we are a member, take us into your body and we will help you remember. Creation is creativity in the midst of play, spend time with us and we will help you on your way.

Taraxaxum spp., Bitterwort, Irish daisy, Lion's Tooth, and Dandelion are a few of our many names. We are many things to many growing things. To you we will become a bitter gift. We offer to you our flowers, leaves, and root, all perfectly edible.

Perhaps

One day a peasant came across his sick horse in a field. The farmer felt compassion and sent his horse away into the forest. Upon hearing the news, his neighbors came to offer their condolences. "What terrible fortune. Your only horse is gone," they said with solemn faces. "Perhaps," said the peasant, "Bad today allows for good tomorrow."

After several days the horse miraculously returned from the forest with three wild horses. Upon hearing the news, his neighbors came to offer their congratulations. "What great fortune you have," they exclaimed.

"Perhaps," said the peasant, "Good today allows for bad tomorrow."

After several days his son tried to ride one of the wild horses. The horse immediately threw the son to the ground, breaking his leg. Upon hearing the news, his neighbors came to offer their condolences. "What terrible fortune. Your only son is injured," they said with solemn faces. "Perhaps," said the peasant, "Bad today allows for good tomorrow."

The following day, soldiers came to the village to draft all the young men into the army. Seeing the son's broken leg, they exempted him from the draft. Upon hearing the news, the peasant's neighbors came to offer their congratulations. "What great fortune you have," they exclaimed. "Perhaps," said the peasant.

Thistle

Gnosis

Oh child, do not despair. We are here, and we have never left. We are always speaking, but you are not always listening. We care for each and every part of this great whole. We care for you. Come close little child, for we know why you despair – you have simply forgotten.

Everything is sacred because everything is divine.

The knowledge of what is surrounds you, because it is you. Gnosis is not just found in our plant world, it is found in every movement of life. There is rock gnosis, sky gnosis, animal gnosis, pain gnosis, joy gnosis, insult gnosis, forgiveness gnosis, birth gnosis, death gnosis, meditation gnosis, and dream gnosis. The list is as infinite as movement. Gnosis is the wisdom that comes with eyes that see further. It is the movements around us and our relationship to these movements that brings about gnosis. Eyes then become whole because they see the whole in everything.

I am, and forever am, that which I am.

Each moment we reflect as in a mirror the movements of the universe. Cells are dying and being reborn right now. Thoughts rise and thoughts fall. With each heartbeat blood goes out and goes back in. Each year experiences summer and winter. Movement carries us along the spiral of life, always into something new.

I am happening.

You are being reborn in every moment, within the space of each preceding thought. All is movement, and you are moving, transforming, progressing, never the same person you were a minute ago. If your mind is chaotic and restless in this moment, it can be still in the next. If your mind is fearful in this moment, it can gain perspective in the next. If your mind is angry and vengeful in this moment, it can rest in peace and forgiveness in the next.

I am becoming that which I am becoming.

The universe is unfolding and we are that which is unfolding. Like the flow of a river, the universe is meandering through the cycles of necessity. When we forget this, we create the necessary counterforce to bring us back to remembrance. As remembering blooms, our behavior flows naturally towards reunion.

Cease to agitate the waters of life and they will become clear.

We have never been separated from the all. We are the all. The gnosis of what we are is simply covered up by necessary illusions. It is the layers of agitated dissonance that we have added to ourselves to help us see ourselves. We are the game creators, playing with creativity.

Reality is a mirror. Look upon the other, and you will see yourself.

As we grow, our perspective grows. As reunion approaches it becomes increasingly difficult to harm another. To harm another is seen clearly as harming our self. To speak evil of another is to speak evil to our self. To pollute the rivers is seen clearly as polluting our veins. To destroy the earth is seen clearly as destroying our body. To change the world is to change our self.

Destroy and destruction will be felt.

Is your world a mess? Then you are the reason for the mess. Is your world full of towers and concrete? Then you are their creators. Reality will become heavy until it is noticed, because reality is the great teacher.

Cities and forests are both teachers.

What is most important is what is happening right now in this moment. You are writing a story. Where this story is going is not important. Where it goes, is where it will go. Laugh and enjoy the process, for everything is as it should be. If you wish to be happy, be happy. If you wish to be sad, be sad. Flow with whatever circumstances come your way. Relate to everything as you would to a great teacher.

Salvation is seeing the other as yourself.

It matters not where you go. It matters where you are, in this moment. Flee from a terrible lot in life, and you will bring that terrible lot with you. Run to wherever you like, and your problems will keep step.

Circumstances follow you because circumstances are you.

Peace is not over there. Happiness is not found through a change of circumstances. Contentment is not gained through more possessing. Remember who you are and you will be peace. Remember who you are and you will be happiness. Remember who you are and you will be contentment. Remembering, you accept whatever is before you, because what is before you has always been you.

Enjoy experience. Grow and learn. Breathe and explore. Mess up and remember. Do not withdraw from activity or try to transcend reality, rather perform your activities with new awareness. Participate more fully, experience more fully. Improvise. Savor the touch, taste, and sounds of chaos and beauty, its cycles, rhythms, and flow. Stand in awe and wonder. Mystery beyond mystery.

We are not the first or the last word in nature. Unfathomable worlds above, unfathomable worlds below.

We are the whole, we are a member, take us into your body and we will help you remember. Creation is creativity in the midst of play, spend time with us and we will help you on your way.

Cirsium spp., Cursed Thistle, Hell Thistle, Milk Thistle, and Way Thistle are a few of our many names. We are many things to many growing things. To you we will become a gift when all other gifts have been turned over. Destroy the world and we will pick up the pieces and offer you ourselves. Rip us apart, and we will multiply our gifts. We offer to you every part of our body as food. We offer to you every part of our body as art. To reject a foe is to reject a friend.

Tiger Above, Tiger Below

A monkey was bouncing through a field when two tigers appeared and started to give chase. The monkey ran to a nearby cliff and jumped onto a hanging vine.

Terrified, the monkey looked up and saw a hungry tiger prowling above him. The monkey looked down and saw the other hungry tiger prowling below. As the monkey pondered what to do he noticed a black and white mouse that was chewing on the vine above him.

As the vine was about to break, the monkey looked in front of him and noticed the stunning foliage and flowers of a Milk Thistle plant. With one hand still firmly holding onto the vine, the monkey let go with the other hand and began to examine this marvelous plant.

How wonderful it appeared!

Growing Meditation

B.A.T.C.H.

As above, so below. As below, so above.

Breathe. We are becoming what we are becoming. In goes the breath. Out goes the breath. A mirror of all that is. Relax.

Sunshine and rain.

Acceptance. Allow what is before you. There are no accidents, there is only learning. Do not despise your teacher. Everything is master. Everything is teacher.

Periods are commas in disguise.

Trust. Process moves us all. Until we are whole, we see but a part. Limited for a reason. We do the best that we can and do not worry about the rest.

Love wears every disguise.

Compassion. Other is a necessary illusion. Everything is divine. What we do to others, we do to ourselves. What we dislike in others, we dislike in ourselves.

Empty cup.

Humility. We know only in part. We meet the other where they are at, not where we are at. We do not preach and we do not force our concepts on others. Concepts are circles. Process is spiraling. We allow each part to become in its own unique way.

www.ingramcontent.com/pod-product-compliance
Lightning Source LLC
Chambersburg PA
CBHW071512150426
43191CB00009B/1504

www.ingramcontent.com/pod-product-compliance
Lightning Source LLC
Chambersburg PA
CBHW071443150426
4319ICB000048/1216